The Metaphysics of Martyrdom

J. Marianne Siegmund

En Route Books and Media, LLC
Saint Louis, MO

⚓ENROUTE
Make the time

En Route Books and Media, LLC
5705 Rhodes Avenue
St. Louis, MO 63109

Contact us at
contactus@enroutebooksandmedia.com

Cover photo by Bartolomé Esteban Murillo,
Mater Dolorosa, (1660). Public Domain.
https://en.wikipedia.org/wiki/Our_Lady_of_Sorrows#/media/File:Dolorosa.jpg

Copyright 2025 J. Marianne Siegmund

ISBN-13: 979-8-88870-456-1 and 979-8-88870-457-8
Library of Congress Control Number:
Available online at http://catalog.loc.gov

All rights reserved. No part of this book may be reproduced, stored in a retrieval system, or transmitted in any form, or by any means, electronic, mechanical, photocopying, or otherwise, without the prior written permission of the author.

In a special way, the person constitutes a privileged locus for the encounter with being, and hence with metaphysical enquiry.

Wherever men and women discover a call to the absolute and transcendent, the metaphysical dimension of reality opens up before them: in truth, in beauty, in moral values, in other persons, in being itself, in God.

Pope Saint John Paul the Great, *Fides et Ratio*, 83

Dedication

To the Sorrowful and Immaculate Heart of Mary
and to
the Holy Innocents
and to
all the martyrs of Holy Mother Church of all time
with special gratitude to
my Guardian Angel

Table of Contents

1: Introduction 1

2: What is Martyrdom? 5

3: Martyrdom and the Dignity of the Human Person 11

4: An Objection to Martyrdom and to the Martyr's Free Will 19

5: Martyrdom and the Holiness of God's Law 31

6: Martyrdom and the Holiness of the Church 37

7: What is Metaphysics? 43

8: What are the Transcendentals? 47

9: The Transcendentals & the Concept of Martyrdom ... 53

10: The Transcendental "The One" & the Notion of Martyrdom 55

11: The Transcendental "The True" Illuminates Martyrdom 65

12: What Can "The Good" Say About Martyrdom? 77

13: Is it Impossible to Attribute Beauty to Martyrdom? . 79

14: The Metaphysics of Martyrdom 85

15: The Martyr's Vision of Reality 93

Bibliography 101

1

Introduction

Metaphysics, or first philosophy, the science of being *qua* being, examines reality in its essential nature. It studies being – reality – insofar as it is being, itself. Since metaphysics is the "solid basis" of theology, and, with death being a "metaphysical thorn lodged in man's being," in this short treatise, I examine the metaphysics of martyrdom.[1] That is, I look at the nature and first principles of martyrdom. What realities are manifest in the very act of martyrdom? How does metaphysics describe its essential nature? In turn, does martyrdom illuminate the first principles of being, itself, in its capacity as being? Does it comment upon being, as a whole?

By martyrdom, I refer to what is commonly called "red martyrdom," or the act of laying down one's life

---

[1] Joseph Cardinal Ratzinger, *The Nature and Mission of Theology: Essays to Orient Theology in Today's Debates*, Translated by Adrian Walker (San Francisco: Ignatius Press, 1995), 22-23.

for the Faith.² As the Greek brings out, *martyr* means *to witness by death*. Thus, "the perfect notion of martyrdom requires that a man suffer death for Christ's sake."³ This is a good but precursory definition of martyrdom, for its very nature must be carefully delineated in order to depict its essential principles and to draw some conclusions.

My plan of action, then, is first to define martyrdom and then to comment upon it. Second, after describing the transcendentals, I illuminate the act of the martyr in light of metaphysics, specifically by a

---

² As St. Thomas explains, "fortitude regards danger of death chiefly, and other dangers consequently; wherefore a person is not called a martyr merely for suffering imprisonment, or exile, or forfeiture of his wealth, except in so far as these result in death" (Thomas Aquinas, *Summa Theologiae* II-II, 124, 4 ad. 3). See also *Catechism of the Catholic Church* Second Edition (Citta del Vaticano: Libreria Editrice Vaticana, 1993), 2473.

³ Thomas Aquinas, *Summa Theologiae* II-II, 124, 4. "As St. Thomas explains, "it belongs to martyrdom that a man bear witness to the faith in showing by deed that he despises all things present, in order to obtain invisible goods to come. Now so long as a man retains the life of the body, he does not show by deed that he despises all things relating to the body. For men are wont to despise both their kindred and all they possess, and even to suffer bodily pain, rather than lose life" (Thomas Aquinas, *Summa Theologiae* II-II, 124, 4).

consideration of the transcendentals. Finally, if martyrdom does indeed highlight certain characteristics of being, as a study of the transcendentals seems to indicate, then it affects people of all time, not only in what they believe, but also in how they live. Consequently, at the end of my treatise, I will draw some practical conclusions regarding the metaphysical claims of martyrdom that concern both belief and life.

2

What is Martyrdom?

A martyr is a "person who chooses…to die, rather than renounce his or her faith" or the moral law.[4] To be sure, the martyr is a witness; he testifies to the truth of what he proclaims by laying down his life for the Faith. Pope Saint John Paul II builds upon this notion of martyrdom in the following passages.

> In one of the most relevant texts, the Holy Father claims that martyrdom is 'fidelity to God's holy law, witnessed to by death' (John Paul II, *Veritatis Splendor* 93). This death affirms 'the inviolability of the moral order [and it] bears splendid witness' (John Paul II, *Veritatis Splendor* 92) to the 'holiness of the Church' (John Paul II, *Veritatis Splendor* 93), to 'the holiness of God's law and to the inviolability of the personal dignity of man' (John

---

[4] John A. Hardon, S.J., *Modern Catholic Dictionary* (Garden City: Doubleday and Company, Inc., 1980), 335.

Paul II, *Veritatis Splendor* 92). Martyrdom 'is also the exaltation of a person's perfect 'humanity' and of true 'life'" (John Paul II, *Veritatis Splendor* 92), and it 'represents the high point of the witness to moral truth' (John Paul II, *Veritatis Splendor* 93).[5]

In the passages delineated above, the Holy Father captures the fundamentals of martyrdom in the first phrase from his Encyclical, *Veritatis Splendor*, where he specifies that it is "fidelity to God's holy law witnessed to by death."[6] Thus, John Paul agrees with and expounds upon the traditional definition of martyrdom, articulated by Saint Thomas Aquinas, as one who "suffer(s) death for Christ's sake."[7]

After highlighting the conventional understanding of martyrdom, the Pope brings into clearer focus the "for Christ's sake" part of the definition. One

---

[5] J. Marianne Siegmund, *The Face of Jesus, the Martyr, and the Reciprocity of Abiding Love: Anthropological Considerations in Spiritual Theology Based Upon the Pontifical Writings of Pope Saint John Paul the Great* (Saint Louis, MO: En Route Books and Media, LLC, 2024), 2-3.

[6] John Paul II, *Veritatis Splendor* 93.

[7] Thomas Aquinas, *Summa Theologiae* II-II, 124, 4.

might note, for example, that "fidelity to God's holy law" further specifies suffering death "for Christ's sake" by bringing the notion of martyrdom into New Testament times. John Paul's definition makes more specific exactly why and how a person forfeits his life "for Christ's sake." For one, it recalls to mind that Jesus Christ has first suffered, died and rose "for *our* sake" (2 Corinthians 5:21) that we might, in turn, risk our lives "for the sake of our Lord Jesus Christ" (Acts 15:26).[8]

Also to be noted is the fact that physical life is a great good. It ought to be safeguarded, preserved and nourished. But spiritual life, one's response to God's gift of faith and the state of sanctifying grace, is higher still. The life of the spirit is a greater good than "simply" the life of the body. Consequently, one's life of union with God through the Holy Spirit, the state of sanctifying grace, is to be preserved at all costs. For no reason, whatsoever, ought a person to depart from the state of grace and succumb to living in mortal sin.

---

[8] *The Holy Bible,* Revised Standard Version Second Catholic Edition (San Francisco, CA: Thomas Nelson Publishing for Ignatius Press, 2006). All Scripture references cite this edition unless otherwise noted.

Accepting death rather than choosing to be unfaithful to the law of God comprises the essence and foundation of martyrdom. The three fundamental elements of martyrdom have thus come to the fore. One's steadfast loyalty (one) unto death (three) rather than transgressing God's holy law in Faith or morals (two) enumerates the three essentials of martyrdom. Without these three points, one does not suffer martyrdom in the manner in which it is normally understood in Catholic Christianity.

From John Paul's longer definition of martyrdom, quoted above, I would like to emphasize three points that further elaborate upon fidelity (one), the law of God (two), and death (three). Expounding upon the notion of fidelity (one), I first highlight the "inviolability of [the person's] personal dignity" to which the martyr's death testifies.[9] Second, I focus upon the law of God and John Paul's notion that the martyr's death bears witness to the holiness of that law through Faith and morals (two).[10] Finally, I make some concluding

---

[9] John Paul II, *Veritatis Splendor* 93; 92.
[10] John Paul II, *Veritatis Splendor* 92.

Chapter 2: What is Martyrdom?

observations regarding martyrdom (death) and the "holiness of the Church" (three).[11]

Naturally, each element is closely interconnected, and one consideration leads to the next. My first task, then, is to describe the concept of martyrdom, itself, in relation to these three ideas: human dignity (fidelity, point one), the law of God (point two) and the holiness of the Church (death "for Christ's sake," which is point three).

---

[11] John Paul II, *Veritatis Splendor* 93.

3

Martyrdom and the Dignity of the Human Person

My first consideration highlights one's fidelity to God and the inviolable dignity of the human person that cannot be transgressed. What is human dignity and how does it apply to martyrdom?

The Fathers of the Second Council of the Vatican teach that the person "has in his heart a law inscribed by God. His dignity lies in observing this law, and by it he will be judged."[12] What *is* good has been decreed by God (cf. Genesis 1:4, 10, 12, 18, 21, 25, 31; 2:16-17). Pursuing the good demands both human freedom and God's grace, for freedom is damaged and weakened by sin.[13] Moreover, each person possesses

---

[12] *Vatican Council II, Volume 1: The Conciliar and Post Conciliar Documents*, New Revised Edition, Austin Flannery, O.P., General Editor. *Gaudium et Spes* [Pastoral Constitution on the Church in the Modern World]. (Northport, NY: Costello Publishing Co., 1996), 16.

[13] Second Vatican Council, *Gaudium et Spes* 17. The Second Vatican Council Fathers indicate as much in the following

dignity because he is created in the image and likeness (Genesis 1:26) of God for eternal union with Him. Achieving that union requires, again, both human freedom in choosing the good and God's grace providing the necessary assistance for the will.[14]

Violating human dignity through killing someone who will not break the law of God is an affront to both God and man. Conversely, the death of the martyr might be considered from the positive perspective. It affirms "the inviolability of the moral order

---

statement. "It is…only in freedom that man can turn himself towards what is good" [Second Vatican Council, *Gaudium et Spes* 17].

[14] *The Canons and Decrees of the Council of Trent*, Translated and Introduced by H. J. Schroeder, O.P., (Rockford, IL: Tan Books and Publishers, Inc., 1978), Sixth Session (January 13, 1547) Decree Concerning Justification Chapter V "The Necessity of Preparation for Justification in Adults and Whence it Proceeds," p. 31-32. The Council notes that, "while God touches the heart of man through the illumination of the Holy Ghost, man himself neither does absolutely nothing while receiving that inspiration, since he can also reject it, nor yet is he able by his own free will and without the grace of God to move himself to justice in His sight. Hence, when it is said in the sacred writings: 'Turn ye to Me, and I will turn to you' (Zechariah 1:3), we are reminded of our liberty; and when we reply: 'Convert us, O Lord, to Thee, and we shall be converted' (Lamentations 5:21), we confess that we need the grace of God."

[and it] bears splendid witness" to the "inviolability of the personal dignity of man" because one refuses to contradict by his words and actions what he knows is true.[15]

Consequently, the martyr's death is a profound act of living in the truth. That act of living in the truth is made visible in the martyr's willingness to die. His death not only upholds human dignity, but also it testifies to the fact that the moral order is transcendent. It is outside of a person, and so it is not made by any human person.

Again, no person can produce the moral law. Its excellence surpasses what anyone can devise, for it is created by God alone. In fact, the "tendency to grant to the individual conscience the prerogative of independently determining the criteria of good and evil and then acting accordingly" indicates "the crisis of truth," for it espouses relativism.[16] As John Paul maintains, "Revelation teaches that the power to decide what is good and what is evil does not belong to man, but to God alone."[17]

---

[15] John Paul II, *Veritatis Splendor* 92.

[16] John Paul II, *Veritatis Splendor* 32.

[17] John Paul II, *Veritatis Splendor* 35.

Living some three centuries before Christ, the pagan Greek philosopher, Aristotle (384-322 BC), sees, using reason alone, that the moral order is not made by the human person. Not only does Aristotle's *Nicomachean* Ethics correspond to natural law, discoverable by human reason, but also, it extends to other works, as well, so much so that Aristotle is dubbed as the "founder of a distinct natural law tradition."[18] Indeed, the moral order is something to which each person must respond, with his own decision, in freedom. No person can manipulate the moral order or set laws in opposition to it by declaring that an action contrary to human nature is acceptable. Thus, rightly does John Paul proclaim that martyrdom is "the high point of the witness to moral truth."[19]

By the very definition of martyrdom, then, one refuses to act contrary to what one knows to be objectively true. One refuses to act against one's conscience. Instead, the person acts in accord with the moral law of God, much of which is discoverable by

---

[18] See, for example, Aristotle's *Politics* and *Rhetoric*. Tony Burns, *Aristotle and Natural Law* (New York, NY: Continuum, 2011), 152.

[19] John Paul II, *Veritatis Splendor* 93.

the light of human reason alone, through the natural law.[20] Those actions bear witness to "inviolability of the personal dignity of man" because he acts in harmony with the end for which he is created.[21] In addition, he reveals by his acts that "law...which is fulfilled in the love of God and of one's neighbor."[22]

To be sure, human freedom manifests "the divine image" in the person.[23] As Sacred Scripture testifies, God's will is to leave man "in the hand of his own counsel" (cf. Ecclesiasticus 15:14 DRA), so that "he might of his own accord seek his Creator and freely attain hist full and blessed perfection by cleaving to Him."[24] What great and fearful power lies in the exercise of one's free will, for by it, one can cooperate with the grace of God or turn aside from it!

---

[20] As Saint Thomas teaches, the natural law is one's participation in the eternal law of God (Thomas Aquinas, *Summa Theologiae* I-II, 91, 2).

[21] John Paul II, *Veritatis Splendor* 92.

[22] Second Vatican Council, *Gaudium et Spes* 16.

[23] John Paul II, *Veritatis Splendor* 34.

[24] *The Holy Bible,* Douay Rheims Version, Revised by Bishop Richard Challoner 1749-1752 (Rockford, IL: Tan Books and Publishers, Inc., 1989). Second Vatican Council, *Gaudium et Spes* 17.

As Thomas Aquinas explains, one turns toward God by an act of the free will. "But free will can only be turned to God, when God turns it, according to Jeremiah 31:18: 'Convert me and I shall be converted, for Thou art the Lord, my God;' and Lamentations 5:21: 'Convert us, O Lord, to Thee, and we shall be converted.'"[25] In sum, grace is necessary for the person's conversion, and God's grace is ever present and readily available. I stress the fact that one needs grace in order to keep the Commandments, fulfill the law of God, and merit eternal life.[26]

What follows is significant, especially concerning the topic of martyrdom. While each person is to be "respected in his own journey in search of the truth, there exists a prior moral obligation, and a grave one at that, to seek the truth and to adhere to it once it is known."[27] One might look to the example of Saint Augustine, who traveled a long and arduous path to conversion. Augustine saw the value in Cicero's exhorta-

---

[25] Thomas Aquinas, *Summa Theologiae* I-II, 109, 6, ad. 1. The Biblical translation is as used in the work of Saint Thomas.

[26] Thomas Aquinas, *Summa Theologiae* I-II, 109, 4-5.

[27] John Paul II, *Veritatis Splendor* 34.

tion to seek wisdom wherever it may be found.[28] Indeed, whatever is true manifests, in some way, the goodness and mercy of God (cf. Philippians 4:8).

To be emphasized is the fact that truth is something outside of the person for which one must diligently search. Once it is found, the person must hold to it with all of one's strength, for one "can find fulfillment only in choosing to enter the truth."[29] The truth must be accepted and entered deeply by everyone. The truth beckons a person. It calls to a person, and it demands adherence. It forbids betrayal, for the betrayal of truth is the destruction of the human person. The martyr, in fact, both accepts the truth and intensely enters into it, with his whole being, by his free acceptance of death.

---

[28] Saint Augustine of Hippo, *Confessions*, Ignatius Critical Editions, Translated by Maria Boulding, O.S.B., Edited by David Vincent Meconi, S.J., Series Editor Joseph Pearce, (San Francisco, CA: Ignatius Press, 2012), Book III, iv, 8.

[29] John Paul II, *Fides et Ratio*, Vatican Translation (Boston, MA: Pauline Books and Media, 1998), 107.

4

An Objection to Martyrdom and to the Martyr's Free Will

One might take exception to highlighting the martyr's free will in adhering to objective truth and to the objective moral order. For example, one might cite the fact that the martyr imitates Christ's non-resistance to "persecutors when they use violence out of hatred or malice against Christ, or His Church, or some revealed truth of the Catholic religion."[30] Because the martyr "does not resist one's persecutors," his death seems somewhat passive.[31] He allows himself to be killed rather than denying the holy law of God. If the person is captured and under duress, one might contend that free will and personal choice cannot be involved.

Can one make the decision to be martyred when death seems so imminent and unavoidable in the first place? One might push the question further still and

---

[30] John A. Hardon, S.J., *Modern Catholic Dictionary*, 335.
[31] John A. Hardon, S.J., *Modern Catholic Dictionary*, 335.

ask whether martyrdom might even be compared to suicide. Since one refuses compliance with conditions that would set the person at liberty, is martyrdom somehow akin to the taking of one's own life?

To be sure, a personal choice *is* involved in martyrdom, even when one is bound in the hands of one's enemies. The martyr accepts the violence perpetrated against oneself, and there certainly *is* a tone of passivity in that acceptance. The action is *being done to* the person. One suffers it.

But in fact, what makes a person a martyr is one's decision during the last moments of one's life, and that (immaterial) act of the will cannot be touched by weapons, prison cells or one's enemies. In fact, it is only visible in words and actions. The very act of *accepting* death still involves a choice and that decision is entirely active.

To emphasize the point, the martyr's seemingly *passive* submission to death demands the parallel and very *active* resolution by which one commits one's whole life and death to God in a sheer act of faith and trust. That act of commitment is a profound living out of the "obedience of faith" (Romans 1:5, 16:26) which "is to be given to God who reveals, an obedi-

Chapter 4: An Objection to Martyrdom

ence by which man commits his whole self freely to God, offering the full submission of intellect and will [and, we might add, he also offers his body and soul, life and death in an act of entrustment] to God who reveals" Himself as a loving Father.[32] Further, as Saint Thomas explains, martyrdom "embraces the highest possible degree of obedience, namely obedience unto death."[33] Jesus Christ, who became "obedient unto death" (Philippians 2:8) is the prime example.[34]

Martyrdom can, in no way, be compared to suicide or to one's own self-destruction in any manner. It is entirely contrary to self-destruction. Rather than taking one's own life in the tragic act of suicide, the martyr upholds and respects his own life even though he is willing to die. Still, one might ask how one's regard for his own life can, in fact, really be the case in martyrdom, given that the person ceases his mortal existence.

---

[32] Second Vatican Council, *Dei Verbum*, 5. As John Paul II observes, one's response to the gift of faith is "the act of entrusting oneself to God… [which is] a moment of fundamental decision…[that] engages the whole person" (John Paul II, *Fides et Ratio* 13).

[33] Thomas Aquinas, *Summa Theologiae* II-II, 124, 3, ad. 2.

[34] Thomas Aquinas, *Summa Theologiae* II-II, 124, 3, ad. 2.

Again, the martyr's acceptance of death indicates that there is a higher law to which he is held accountable. Adherence to this law, written on his heart, "is the very dignity of man; according to it he will be judged."[35] The martyr is convicted of the truth of the Faith and the moral code so much so that he will not lay them aside to preserve even the great good of his own bodily life. In sum, while human life is a very great treasure, obedience to the law of God is an even greater good in the hierarchy of goods. It ranks above all else, and there is no comparison to it. The objective moral law is summarized in the Ten Commandments.

Martyrdom is not comparable to suicide for the following reasons. First, in suicide, one takes one's own life by an act of violence against oneself. In martyrdom, one accepts violence and death to oneself instigated by another because of the greater good to which one's act of martyrdom testifies: the objective orders of truth and the good. Second, in suicide, there is despair and a sense of hopelessness regarding life. One gives up, as a coward, in the face of suffering. In

---

[35] Second Vatican Council, *Gaudium et Spes* 16.

martyrdom, one is filled with courage and a willingness to endure any kind of suffering with a sense of hope in the life to come.

By way of illustration, consider the dialogue between Pope Saint Sixtus II (d. August 6, 258) and his faithful Deacon, Saint Lawrence (225-258). Both were martyred during the persecution of Valerian in 258. The dialogue between the two martyrs, though lengthy, deserves quotation in full. It attests to their courage, their willingness to suffer for the greatest good, and their undaunted hope in the life to come. In the words of each martyr, we see the sheer level of holiness and detachment from this world evident in their words. Both martyrs look to God and to His Heavenly kingdom, intent on the final goal of their labor in life. Consequently, martyrdom testifies to all the opposites of suicide. I recount the dialogue between Sixtus II and Lawrence from the text of Saint Ambrose (c. 339-397), who was born about ninety years after the martyrdoms of Sixtus and Lawrence occurred.

> Saint Lawrence wept when he saw his Bishop, Sixtus, led out to his martyrdom. He wept not

because he was being let out to die but because he would survive Sixtus. He cried out to him in a loud voice: 'Where are you going Father, without your son? Where do you hasten to, holy Bishop, without your Deacon? You cannot offer sacrifice without a minister. Father, are you displeased with something in me? Do you think me unworthy? Show us a sign that you have found a worthy minister. Do you not wish that he to whom you gave the Lord's Blood and with whom you have shared the Sacred Mysteries should spill his own blood with you? Beware that in your praise your own judgment should not falter. Despise the pupil and shame the Master. Do not forget that great and famous men are victorious more in the deeds of their disciples than in their own. Abraham made sacrifice of his own son; Peter instead sent Stephen. Father, show us your own strength in your sons; sacrifice him whom you have raised, to attain eternal reward in that glorious company, secure in your judgment."[36]

Before turning to the response of Pope Sixtus, note the longing in Lawrence's words. One can almost hear his pleading tone as he greatly desires to bear witness to God by the shedding of his blood. Lawrence is entirely focused upon the life to come. Since martyrdom is the means to arrive there, he earnestly pines for it. While martyrdom entails bodily death, it likewise includes spiritual life with God and with the blessed ones in Heaven. As well, note the fact that Lawrence longs not for death, but to receive the martyr's crown. Necessarily, that implies death, but the focus, the object of the act, is shedding one's blood to bear witness to objective truth, to the objective moral order, to Christ Jesus and to His holy Church. Great is the hope of Saint Lawrence, and he hopes for eternal life.

---

[36] Ambrose, *De Officiis* (cap. 41, nn. 205-206-207) quoted in Fr. Francesco Moraglia, "Saint Lawrence Proto-Deacon of the Roman Church," which is available at the Vatican website here: https://press.vatican.va/roman_curia/congregations/cclergy/documents/rc_con_cclergy_doc_19022000_slaw_en.html.

Lawrence also considers it a high honor to be called to martyrdom. He wants it for himself that he might share in it together with his beloved Holy Father, whom he served so faithfully during life. In sum, Lawrence's words express both sorrow at not being martyred in the present moment together with the Holy Father and they articulate his ardent yearning to share that same kind of death through which he might "glorify God" (John 21:19).

With the following words, Pope Saint Sixtus II responds to Lawrence's plea to follow him immediately in holy martyrdom. Note the genuine love, esteem and solicitude that the Holy Father has for Lawrence, as he is ever intent upon his faithful servant's eternal reward. In no uncertain terms, Sixtus replies that Lawrence, relying upon the grace of God, is entirely strong enough to undergo martyrdom by himself, without his paternal solicitude on hand to encourage him. Sixtus responds as follows.

> I will not leave you; I will not abandon you, my son. More difficult trials are kept for you. A shorter race is set for us who are older. For you who are young a more glorious triumph

over tyranny is reserved. Soon, you will see. Cry no more; after three days you will follow me. It is fitting that such an interval should be set between Bishop and Levite. It would not have been fitting for you to die under the guidance of a martyr, as though you needed help from him. Why do want to share in my martyrdom? I leave its entire inheritance to you. Why do need me present? The weak pupil precedes the master, the strong, who have no further need of instruction, follow and conquer without him. Thus, Elijah left Elisha. I entrust the success of my strength to you.[37]

With these words, one witnesses the Holy Father's unqualified confidence that Lawrence will resolutely hold fast to God's grace in the upcoming trial of his own martyrdom. When the Holy Father says, "I leave its entire inheritance to you," Sixtus implies Lawrence's confidence in God's grace. Rather than the two suffering together, Sixtus foretells that his strong

---

[37] Ambrose, *De Officiis* in Moraglia, "Saint Lawrence Proto-Deacon of the Roman Church."

"pupil," relying upon the grace of God, will "follow and conquer without him [Sixtus]."[38] Lawrence has learned his lesson well. He does not look to Sixtus for assistance, but for a share in martyrdom. With the grace of God, Lawrence is strong enough to endure the suffering martyrdom demands on his own, and he will, indeed, shed his blood for the sake of Christ and His Church, which is his only and ardent desire.

Like other martyrs, Lawrence is attracted to the "absolute Good, which…beckons us; it is the echo of a call from God who is the origin and goal" of every person's life.[39] Even more, the martyr bears witness to God and to other transcendent realities, such as the true and the good. In the willing acceptance of death, the martyr decides to allow it in order to hold fast to an even greater good, which is the law higher than oneself: objective truth and the objective moral order. The martyr's decision, then, bears witness to "the holiness of God's law" of belief and moral action.[40] The

---

[38] Ambrose, *De Officiis* in Moraglia, "Saint Lawrence Proto-Deacon of the Roman Church." The grace of God is absolutely essential, and that is why I stress it in this section. The Catholic Church is not Pelagian.

[39] John Paul II, *Veritatis Splendor* 7.

[40] John Paul II, *Veritatis Splendor* 92.

person refuses to act contrary to the truth and the good. As a consequence, the martyr also preserves one's own moral integrity as a subject of human action.

Sacrificing one's life speaks loudly because it speaks definitively. In effect, the martyr refuses to live a lie. With living a lie or dying being the only options given to the person by the perpetrators of martyrdom, the martyr readily chooses death not for some morbid reason, but rather because he is honest; he fully desires to live in the truth. He rejects the temptation to deny what he knows is true. Instead of living an unexamined life, as Socrates once cautioned against, the martyr assesses his life when a verdict upon human action is required.[41] Recognizing a grave evil, he examines his conscience, and bears witness to the truth with an unambiguous judgment. Indeed, for human life to be lived rightly, it must accord with the dictates of the well-formed conscience,

---

[41] *The Collected Dialogues of Plato Including the Letters*, Bollingen Series LXXI, Edited by Edith Hamilton and Huntington Cairns, Translated by Hugh Tredennick, et al., (Princeton, New Jersey: Princeton University Press, 1980), *Apology*, 38a5–6. Literally "ὁ δὲ ἀνεξέταστος βίος οὐ βιωτὸς ἀνθρώπῳ" might be translated as "but the unexamined life is not lived by man."

adhering to objective truth. One cannot live a lie without serious ramifications to one's own humanity.

One's sacred dignity as a human person is intimately connected with both one's free will and conscience, yet neither freedom nor conscience is absolute. While each person possesses dignity, having been created in the image and likeness of God (Genesis 1:26), he has more or less dignity insofar as he uses his free will in accord with the will of God.[42] Thus, the sacred dignity of the person points toward the second element of martyrdom, which is the holy law of God.[43]

---

[42] Second Vatican Council, *Gaudium et Spes* 16.
[43] John Paul II, *Veritatis Splendor* 92.

5

Martyrdom and the Holiness of God's Law

As I note above, the martyr testifies to the inviolability of the moral law and to human dignity by choosing to endure martyrdom. He obeys his well-formed conscience, which bears witness to objective truth and to the objective moral order. The law of God is holy, and it is not to be violated for any reason.

Again, I stress the point. By an act of his free will, the martyr bears witness to God's holy law. In fact, such cooperation of the person's freedom with God's law might be described as a "participated theonomy," for one's "free obedience to God's law effectively implies that human reason and human will participate in God's wisdom and providence" by the "light of natural reason and of Divine Revelation."[44] Rather than one assembling a moral code for the human race, each person is called to participate, in freedom, in the

---

[44] John Paul II, *Veritatis Splendor* 41.

holy law of God. The human person is not his own autonomous lawgiver. Consequently, rather than law being an arbitrary human construct, it is instead an "expression of divine wisdom: by submitting to the law, freedom submits to the truth of creation."[45] God Himself gives mankind the moral law as a gift for his own peace and happiness.

What is the human free will? In the *Modern Catholic Dictionary*, one learns that free will is the "power of the will to determine itself and to act of itself, without compulsion from within or coercion from without. It is the faculty of an intelligent being to act or not act, to act this way or another way."[46] One of the amazing characteristics regarding martyrdom is that there *is* exterior coercion, even to the point of grave suffering, deprivation and death. Yet, the martyr freely acts in accord with the objective moral order by refusing to deny or to act against it. Therefore, the martyr is truly free, and he acts in full freedom. Yet, human freedom is not absolute, for again, only God

---

[45] John Paul II, *Veritatis Splendor* 41.
[46] John A. Hardon, S.J., *Modern Catholic Dictionary*, 221.

has "the power to decide what is good and what is evil."[47]

The martyr's unwillingness to violate the holy law of God touches upon both human freedom and the limits of human freedom. Each person is free. Moreover, the person "possesses an extremely far-reaching freedom, since he can eat 'of every tree of the garden.' [Yet, human freedom is not absolute; it]…is not unlimited: it must halt before the 'tree of the knowledge of good and evil,' for it is called to accept the moral law given by God."[48] Although it is wide-ranging, there are limits to human freedom.[49]

While freedom is a great good, it is only genuinely good when it is, in fact, limited; one can want "more than it is good for us to have in relation to our fellowmen, and [one can want] more than we have any right to" possess.[50] Again, one is *not* one's own sovereign

---

[47] John Paul II, *Veritatis Splendor* 35.

[48] John Paul II, *Veritatis Splendor* 35.

[49] John Paul II, *Veritatis Splendor* 35.

[50] Mortimer J. Adler, *Six Great Ideas* (New York, NY: Touchstone Simon & Schuster Inc., 1997), 137. In contrast, Adler notes other goods that are unlimited. For example, we can never "seek or obtain more [justice, knowledge, or wisdom] than is good for us" (137).

lawgiver. Rather, the law to which one must adhere is given by God (the Ten Commandments) and "human freedom finds its authentic and complete fulfillment precisely in the acceptance of that law."[51] One is fulfilled precisely by something greater than oneself that is outside of oneself. The person is incapable of making oneself completely happy. He simply cannot do it. Consequently, the martyr is not only free, but his free decision "finds its authentic and complete fulfillment" in accepting the holy Law of God and in suffering death rather than adhering to a lie. The truth impels him onward, for "He who says 'I know Him' but disobeys His Commandments is a liar, and the truth is not in him" (1 John 2:4).

As mentioned above, just as human freedom is not absolute, neither is conscience. The conscience is an act of the practical reason, which applies knowledge to a particular situation.[52] It is an *act* and not a

---

[51] John Paul II, *Veritatis Splendor* 35. The Holy Father describes the person's freedom as a participated theonomy whereby one's "human reason and human will participate in God's wisdom and providence" [John Paul II, *Veritatis Splendor* 41].

[52] Thomas Aquinas, *Questiones Disputatae de Veritate: Truth*, Translated by James V. McGlynn, S.J., (Chicago, IL:

feeling or a hunch. Conscience is not an emotion. Its act is "to apply the universal knowledge of the good in a specific situation and thus to express a judgment about the right conduct to be chosen here and now."[53] Conscience adheres to the objective moral order. In one's conscience, a person finds "a law which he has not laid upon himself but which he must obey."[54] Something is not true because it originates in the conscience; it is true because it adheres to the "universal truth about the good," which is called the moral order, the Decalogue and the law of God.[55]

While one is certainly to follow one's conscience, a person likewise has the primary obligation to form one's conscience in accord with truth, which is objective, and in harmony with the moral order, which is also objective. One's moral judgment is true if it adheres to moral norms that one does not create but receives from the Eternal Lawgiver. Thus, while the power of human freedom, upheld by grace under the

---

Henry Regnery Company, 1953), 17, 1-2. https://isidore.co/aquinas/QDdeVer17.htm; *Summa Theologiae* I, 79, 13. See also: John Paul II, *Veritatis Splendor* 32.

[53] John Paul II, *Veritatis Splendor* 32.
[54] Second Vatican Council, *Gaudium et Spes* 16.
[55] John Paul II, *Veritatis Splendor* 32.

cruelty of martyrdom, bears witness to the holiness of God's law, the act of conscience testifies to the holiness of the Church, which provides the guidelines, principles and content to which conscience must adhere.[56] Acts of the well-formed conscience, therefore, reflect the holiness of Holy Mother Church. It is to this subject that I now turn.

---

[56] In broad terms, the Church is "the faithful of the whole world" (John A. Hardon, S.J., *Modern Catholic Dictionary*, 105). More specifically, she is "a union of human beings who are united by the profession of the same Christian Faith, and by participation in the same sacraments under the direction of their lawful pastors, especially by the vicar of Christ on earth, the Bishop of Rome" (Kenneth Baker, S.J., *Fundamentals of Catholicism*, Vol. 3 (San Francisco, CA: Ignatius Press, 1983), 91.

6

Martyrdom and the Holiness of the Church

In speaking about the holiness of the Church, I note that Catholic theology teaches that the Church is holy for four reasons. As the Second Vatican Council document, *Lumen Gentium*, explains, the Church is holy in her origin both because her founder is Jesus Christ and because she is animated by the Holy Spirit.[57] Second, the Church is holy because her purpose is holy: "the glory of God and the salvation" of the human race.[58] Third, the Church is holy because the means used to attain her purpose are holy, for example, Sacred Scripture, the sacraments, and sacramentals,[59] and finally, the Church is holy in her members, that is, the saints.[60]

---

[57] Second Vatican Council, *Lumen Gentium* 5, 9.
[58] Kenneth Baker, S.J., *Fundamentals of Catholicism*, 141. Second Vatican Council, *Lumen Gentium* 9-10; 14.
[59] Second Vatican Council, *Lumen Gentium* 11.
[60] Second Vatican Council, *Lumen Gentium* 40-1; 48.

> She is holy in her purpose which is the glory of God and the salvation of men. The means she uses to attain her goal are holy: the Word of God contained in the Bible, the sacraments, the Holy Sacrifice of the Mass, her religious communities and her sacramentals. The Church is also holy in her fruits or results, that is, she is known from the holiness of those men and women who, filled with the faith of the Church, make full use of the means of grace and holiness put at their disposal by the Church. These are the 'saints' of the Church, both canonized and uncanonized.[61]

The Old Testament figure of Susanna is an image of the Church, which is unjustly persecuted and yet still victorious. The image of Susanna serves as an example of my third point, which is that the martyr bears witness to the holiness of the Church. Against the malice and deceit of the wicked judges, Susanna decisively chooses *not* to sin (Daniel 13:22-23). She

---

[61] Kenneth Baker, S.J., *Fundamentals of Catholicism*, 141.

knows and fully acknowledges that refraining from "sin in the sight of the Lord" will result in falling into the hands of her enemies who will work to bring about her death (Daniel 13:22-23).

> [By] preferring to 'fall innocent' into the hands of the judges, [Susanna] bears witness not only to her faith and trust in God but also to her obedience to the truth and to the absoluteness of the moral order. By her readiness to die a martyr, she proclaims that it is not right to do what God's law qualifies as evil in order to draw some good from it. Susanna chose for herself the 'better part:' hers was a perfectly clear witness, without any compromise, to the truth about the good and to the God of Israel. By her acts, she revealed the holiness of God.[62]

---

[62] John Paul II, *Veritatis Splendor* 91. To reiterate, the point that John Paul makes is that one must "form one's acts according to norms based on the authentic highest good and not on a lesser good" [Adrian J. Reimers, *Truth About the Good: Moral Norms in the Thought of John Paul II* (Ave Maria, FL: Sapientia Press of Ave Maria University, 2011), 136-137]. One is obliged to keep the Commandments even when doing so directly results

Susanna and every martyr highlight the holiness of the Church by adhering to her teaching over and above all other things. This singular manifestation of detachment from the world and from all that is within it is noteworthy. While there are many good things in the world, such as freedom, human relationships and the goods of the earth, all these pale in comparison with the greatest good. In the various decisions of life, one cannot set aside the highest good, the law of God, to satisfy lesser goods. Those lesser goods will not fulfill a person. Seeking the finite goods of the earth results in emptiness, discomfort and unrest within oneself. Leaving behind these finite, limited goods, the martyr's detachment from them radiates a readiness to embrace true life, which also mirrors the holiness of the Church.[63]

Having examined the nature of martyrdom and several realities that are manifest in the very act of martyrdom, such as activity as opposed to passivity,

---

in forfeiting one's bodily life. That is exactly what the sacrament of Confirmation strengthens one to fulfill.

[63] Ignatius of Antioch, *Early Christian Writings: The Apostolic Fathers*, Translated by Maxwell Staniforth, (New York, NY: Dorset Press, 1986), The Epistle to the Romans, 6

in addition to freedom, grace, and conscience, I now strive to pinpoint its first principles with the help of metaphysics, and the transcendentals, in particular. After defining the nature of metaphysics and the transcendentals, I focus upon the act of the martyr at the moment of death in light of my work in metaphysics with the transcendentals.

7

What is Metaphysics?

By *metaphysics*, I mean the traditional understanding of that branch of philosophy concerning the "science of being, as being."[64] Thus, one first asks, what is being? Noting the different ways in which one can understand being, I make the following distinction. One might regard being in its broadest sense as "what is or that which exists, that is, reality."[65] I highlight the distinction between that which is first grasped by the intellect (i.e., being as that which exists or being in general) and that which is the subject of metaphysics.[66]

---

[64] John A. Hardon, S.J., *Modern Catholic Dictionary*, 349.

[65] Ralph M. McInerny and Jeffrey Dirk Wilson, "Being" Vol. 1 p. 169-175 in *New Catholic Encyclopedia Supplement 2012-2013: Ethics and Philosophy*, Ed. Robert L. Fastiggi. 4 vols. (Detroit, MI: Gale, 2013), 169.

[66] Ralph M. McInerny and Jeffrey Dirk Wilson, "Being" in *New Catholic Encyclopedia Supplement 2012-2013: Ethics and Philosophy*, 169-171.

In my work, I first emphasize being in general, as that which is first grasped by the intellect. Second, I highlight being insofar as it is the subject of metaphysics, that is, what is immaterial, as opposed to physics, which studies "being insofar as it is material and changeable."[67]

Metaphysics involves the "principles of being, the transcendental properties of being…the study of what is real…[and] what being (or existence) itself is."[68] Because it studies the "first principles of being," *metaphysics* may also be called "the philosophy of first causes."[69] Additionally called *ontology*, this science "may also consider what it means to be, what sorts of entities are countenanced, and what kinds of ultimate presuppositions or principles are held or obtained."[70] In that light, contemporary fundamental

---

[67] Ralph M. McInerny and Jeffrey Dirk Wilson, "Being" in *New Catholic Encyclopedia Supplement 2012-2013: Ethics and Philosophy*, 171.

[68] James G. Murphy, S.J., "Metaphysics" Vol. 3 p. 1186 in *New Catholic Encyclopedia Supplement 2012-2013: Ethics and Philosophy*, Ed. Robert L. Fastiggi. 4 vols. (Detroit, MI: Gale, 2013), 1186.

[69] John A. Hardon, S.J., *Modern Catholic Dictionary*, 349.

[70] Daniel O. Dahlstrom and Marco Lamanna, "Ontology" Vol. 3 p. 1103-08 in *New Catholic Encyclopedia Supplement*

theologian, David L. Schindler (1943-2022), describes metaphysics as "some vision of reality inclusive of ideas about being, man, and God."[71]

Having examined the decisive act of the martyr in terms of activity as opposed to passivity, in addition to freedom, grace, and conscience, one might now inquire into that "vision of reality" which the martyr manifests. To construct an answer, I examine martyrdom in conjunction with the qualities or characteristics of being, itself, through a brief study of the transcendentals. Upon reflection of the martyr in light of the transcendentals, I articulate the vision of reality that he illuminates. That metaphysic builds the next tier of an answer to my question concerning whether the nature of martyrdom comments upon the whole

---

2012-2013: Ethics and Philosophy, Ed. Robert L. Fastiggi. 4 vols. (Detroit, MI: Gale, 2013), 1103. While *metaphysics* and *ontology* have long since been held as synonyms, today analytic philosophy distinguishes between the two. *Ontology* is "concerned with the question of 'what there is,' whereas *metaphysics* is concerned with the question 'what it is' (Varzi 2011)" (1104). Since I am principally concerned with the question of what martyrdom is, I use the term, *metaphysics*, rather than *ontology*.

[71] David L. Schindler, *Ordering Love: Liberal Societies and the Memory of God* (Grand Rapids, MI and Cambridge, U.K.: William B. Eerdmans Publishing Company, 2011), 437.

of being. My first task, then, is to examine the transcendentals.

8

What are the Transcendentals?

As scholastic philosophy teaches, the transcendentals are "those qualities that are common to all things whatsoever, and to all differences between things."[72] The transcendentals are "not restricted to any category, class, or individual," and they are convertible with being, itself.[73] In other words, the transcendentals are "the properties of real being as being."[74] They describe the nature of being, or reality itself.

The transcendentals explicate the concept of being (i.e., being in general) in its "most common or most general notions, such as the one (unum), the

---

[72] John A. Hardon, S.J., *Modern Catholic Dictionary*, 544.

[73] John A. Hardon, S.J., *Modern Catholic Dictionary*, 544.

[74] Jan A. Aertsen and Wouter Goris, "Transcendentals" Vol. 4 pages 1556-1560 in *New Catholic Encyclopedia Supplement 2012-2013: Ethics and Philosophy*, Ed. Robert L. Fastiggi. 4 vols. (Detroit, MI: Gale, 2013), 1559.

true (verum), and the good (bonum)."[75] In other words, every being (ens) that *is*, "is one, true, and good. Yet the words are not merely synonyms for the same thing; they differ conceptually."[76] Moreover, the transcendentals are, in fact, the "most basic conceptions of the intellect. As such, they are the self-evident termini, in which the analytic or resolving movement of the intellect ends, and they are the indubitable and most certain starting points of cognition."[77] From such a description, one can see that the transcendentals consider being in general, as that which is first conceived by the intellect, rather than being as the subject of metaphysics. And yet, the transcendentals, themselves, form part of metaphysics.

---

[75] Jan A. Aertsen and Wouter Goris, "Transcendentals" in *New Catholic Encyclopedia Supplement 2012-2013: Ethics and Philosophy*, 1556. "'The one' formally adds the negation of division to being, 'the true' and 'the good,' an extrinsic denomination, but what is explicated through them is the nature of being with respect to its perfection or integrity" (1559).

[76] Jan A. Aertsen and Wouter Goris, "Transcendentals" in *New Catholic Encyclopedia Supplement 2012-2013: Ethics and Philosophy*, 1557.

[77] Jan A. Aertsen and Wouter Goris, "Transcendentals" in *New Catholic Encyclopedia Supplement 2012-2013: Ethics and Philosophy*, 1557.

Chapter 8: What are the Transcendentals? 49

One might ponder the transcendentals in order to consider the nature of being and the way in which being is related, one to another. Even more, the "doctrines of the transcendentals do not merely give an extension on account of the most general properties of being, but also an account of the inner relations and order between these notions."[78] In other words, the transcendentals show how beings are connected.

Although Plato[79] and pre-Socratic metaphysician, Heraclitus,[80] acknowledge beauty as a

---

[78] Jan A. Aertsen and Wouter Goris, "Transcendentals" in *New Catholic Encyclopedia Supplement 2012-2013: Ethics and Philosophy*, 1557.

[79] Serving as examples, Plato speaks of beauty as a form in the following dialogues: *Phaedo* 65d, 75d, 100b; *Cratylus* 439c, and *Republic* 476b, 493e, and 507b. Elsewhere, Plato, recounting his dialogue with Socrates, discusses the "form of the good" (Plato, *Republic* 454c-d, 508 a-c). While Plato acknowledges that the truth and knowledge are important, the good ranks higher; the "good is yet more prized" (Plato, *Republic* 508d-e).

[80] "Heraclitus (Diels and Krans, *Die Fragmente der Vorsokratiker* [1951-1952], 22 B 102, 1:173) and Socrates (Xenophon., *Mem.* 3.8.5, 7) assert that everything is both good and beautiful. Plato teaches the same doctrine in two ways: indirectly, by teaching that whatever is good is beautiful (*Lysis* 216d, *Tim.* 87c) and that everything participates in the good (*Rep.* 517c); and directly, by holding that everything is made both good and beautiful (*Tim.* 53b)" [Francis J. Kovach and Margaret

transcendental, its inclusion in later philosophical thought is both nuanced and debated.[81] Like many others who hold to the classical view, such as Joseph Cardinal Ratzinger and DC Schindler, I believe that beauty should rightly be considered a transcendental.[82] Since arguing the point lies beyond the scope of

---

I. Hughes, "Beauty as a Transcendental" Vol. 1 pages 162-166 in *New Catholic Encyclopedia Supplement 2012-2013: Ethics and Philosophy*, Ed. Robert L. Fastiggi. 4 vols. (Detroit, MI: Gale, 2013), 162].

[81] See, for example, the following articles. Jan A. Aertsen, 1991. "Beauty in the Middle Ages: A Forgotten Transcendental?" *Medieval Philosophy & Theology* Vol. 1, pages 68-97. Available online: https://doi.org/10.5840/medievalpt199115 David C. Schindler, "Love and Beauty: The 'Forgotten Transcendental' in Thomas Aquinas" *Communio: International Catholic Review* 44 (Summer 2017). Anthony Michael Miller, "The Transcendental Status of Beauty: Evaluating the Debate among Neo-Thomistic Philosophers" *Religions* 15, no. 10: 1207 (2024). https://doi.org/10.3390/rel15101207.

[82] Congregation for the Doctrine of the Faith, Message of His Eminence Cardinal Joseph Ratzinger: To the Communion and Liberation (CL) Meeting at Rimini (24-30 August 2002) *"The Feeling of Things, the Contemplation of Beauty."* David C. Schindler, "Love and Beauty: The 'Forgotten Transcendental' in Thomas Aquinas" *Communio: International Catholic Review* 44 (Summer 2017). In addition, DC Schindler, in The Edna and George McMahon Aquinas Lecture (2016) brings out the nuance that, while Aquinas holds that love is the primary

Chapter 8: What are the Transcendentals?

this project, I simply accept the inclusion of beauty as a transcendental and reserve argumentation for further dialogue elsewhere. Admitting the varying lists of transcendentals, my discussion focuses upon the one (unum), the true (verum), the good (bonum), and the beautiful (pulchrum).[83]

---

passion (emotion) of the soul, and he links it with goodness, he also maintains that love is more closely associated with beauty (YouTube, https://www.youtube.com/watch?v=ei6eRK28oac). The two perfectly coincide.

[83] The classic list of the transcendentals includes the following: thing (res), being (ens), something (aliquid), the one (unum), the true (verum), the good (bonum), "and, according to some philosophers, the beautiful (pulchrum)" (John A. Hardon, S.J., *Modern Catholic Dictionary*, 544).

9

The Transcendentals and the Concept of Martyrdom

A brief presentation of the four transcendentals, particularly in their relation to the concept of martyrdom, comprises the next step. Explicating the metaphysical meaning of martyrdom with the aid of the transcendentals will enable me to depict the vision of reality to which the martyr testifies. In other words, applying the transcendentals to the nature of martyrdom reveals key insights upon not only the human person, God and the world, but also upon the whole of being.

10

The Transcendental "The One" and the Notion of Martyrdom

The first transcendental I consider is the one (unum). To begin, I note the distinction between the metaphysical meaning of "one" and the mathematical meaning of "one." When speaking of the mathematical "one," Aristotle, for example, highlights it as "the first measure of a kind, and above all of quantity."[84] Saint Thomas explains the distinction as follows.

> [T]he one that is convertible with being adds only something conceptual to being, i.e. the negation of division; whereas the one that is the principle of number adds something real, i.e. the relation to a measure, as a consequence of which the extension of the concept

---

[84] Aristotle, *Metaphysics* X, c. 1, 1052 b 18–19.

of being is narrowed down to the category of quantity."[85]

For my purposes here, I consider the one as a transcendental, and, therefore, as that which negates separation. By "the one," then, I mean "'indivisibility as the proper meaning of unity.'"[86] If something is one, it cannot be divided or separated from what it is. The notion of the "one" signifies "that which is whole or undivided in itself, and different or distinct from every other."[87]

There are several ways in which a person might apply oneness, or indivisibility to the martyr, and I think predication can assist. In the Book of *Categories*, Aristotle distinguishes between what is "said of" a subject, or an essential predication, such as Socrates is a man, and that which is "present in" the subject, or

---

[85] Goris Wouter and Jan Aertsen, "Medieval Theories of Transcendentals," *The Stanford Encyclopedia of Philosophy* (Fall 2019 Edition), Edward N. Zalta (editor), https://plato.stanford.edu/archives/fall2019/entries/transcendentals-medieval/, 7.

[86] Goris Wouter and Jan Aertsen, "Medieval Theories of Transcendentals," *The Stanford Encyclopedia of Philosophy*, 7.

[87] John A. Hardon, S.J., *Modern Catholic Dictionary*, 390.

an accidental predication, such as Socrates is wise.[88] The martyr's death is both "said of" a subject and "present in" a subject, so it would be charted as a universal non-substance.[89] (The martyr's death is not a universal substance because it is present in subjects. If martyrdom is "present in" something, then that thing is the substance and martyrdom is a non-substance.)

Applying the concept of Aristotelian predication to the metaphysical notion of "the one," the following illustration subsists. Since the martyr's death is "said of" someone then it is a universal (not a particular) and it is an indivisible concept. While the martyr's death may be predicated of many individuals, the concept remains one and undivided in itself (i.e., the metaphysical understanding of "one"). Martyrdom is

---

[88] Aristotle, *Categories*, 1a17-1b9.

[89] Aristotle, *Categories*, 1a17-1b9. If martyrdom is "said of" something, then it is a universal. If it is not "said of" anything, it is a particular. If martyrdom is "present in" something, then that thing is the substance, and martyrdom is a non-substance. If the martyr's death is not present in anything then it is a substance. But the martyr's death can indeed be "said of" many people. This study makes me wonder whether Aristotle's list of categories may be understood as his list of transcendentals.

a universal because each instance has certain recognizable qualities or characteristics. As noted earlier, those qualities are one's fidelity (one) unto death (three) rather than transgressing God's holy law (two). The martyr's death is not a substance, but an accident, for there are numerous ways to expire.[90] Martyrdom, then, is one way a person dies.

Considering "one" from the mathematical perspective as "quantity," one acknowledges that there are many instances of martyrdom (the Church has countless martyrs) and there are many ways of slaying the martyr. The concept of martyrdom, however, is, at bottom, one. The martyr's death aligns with the transcendental of "the one" not because there is only one instance of martyrdom in the Church, nor because there is only one way of killing a person. Instead, the martyr's death is "said of" the person who is martyred; it inheres in the subject (an accident, rather than a substance). The martyr's death is one and indivisible with the person in whom it inheres; it cannot be separated from the martyr, himself.

---

[90] Aristotle defines "substance" as "that which is neither predicable of a subject nor present in a subject" (Aristotle, *Categories*, 2a11-13).

Chapter 10: The Transcendental "The One"

What "the one," particularly as applied to the martyr's death, says about *being* is that it can be understood as a universal non-substance, since it is both "said of" a subject and "present in" a subject. The martyr's death is a single, indivisible reality. The concepts of *martyr* and *martyrdom* cannot be divided, for the martyr is characterized as such by his death. Concerning the martyr, then, "the one" teaches that *martyrdom* is what makes the martyr a martyr. Oneness is indivisible from the death the person dies.

To be sure, the very essence of martyrdom denotes the impossibility of it being divided from the moment of death. In other words, martyrdom, considered from the metaphysical perspective of the transcendental, "the one," is that moment in history when a person willingly undergoes death rather than denying Faith or morals. A person who is martyred is described not according to what he did in his life. Rather, he is characterized by his free-will decision at the moment of death. This fact is to be noted, therefore, and it signifies that death is somehow a defining moment of one's life.[91] There is one God (Deuteronomy 6:4), who alone is worthy of everything a person is and has and can be (cf. Apocalypse 4:11; 5:12). The "one thing" about which the Scriptures speak is profound union with God and the martyr manifests that reality by the death he willingly undergoes (Psalm 27:4; Luke 10:42).

Further contributions of the transcendental "the one" to the notion of martyrdom are many, but I would like to focus upon the martyr's single heartedness, whereby his entire focus is upon God. The greater g/Good for whom he dies is such a strong magnet that it gathers up the entire life, death and all one's thoughts together in a single unity; the martyr refuses to contradict what he knows is true and good. Single heartedness denotes purity of heart, and, in fact, both describe a merciful heart, as Isaac of Ninevah (i.e., Saint Isaac the Syrian, c. 613-c. 700) explains in the following passage.

---

[91] Death is, indeed, the defining moment of one's life and that is true whether or not one is a martyr. The moment of death sums up one's life and – hopefully – hands one's life back to the Heavenly Father in an act of gratitude.

And what is the sum of purity? A heart full of mercy unto the whole created nature.... And what is a merciful heart? He replied: The burning of the heart unto the whole creation, man, fowls and beasts, demons, and whatever exists so that by the recollection and the sight of them, the eyes shed tears on account of the force of mercy which moves the heart by great compassion. Then the heart becomes weak and it is not able to bear hearing or examining injury or any insignificant suffering of anything in the creation. And therefore even in behalf of the irrational beings and the enemies of truth and even in behalf of those who do harm to it, at all times he offers prayers with tears that they may be guarded and strengthened; even in behalf of the kinds of reptiles, on account of his great compassion which is poured out in his heart without measure, after the example of God.[92]

---

[92] Isaac of Ninevah, *Oeuvres Spirituelles* (Brussels: Desclée de Brouwer, 1981), 81st Discourse, p. 395 quoted in Jacques Philippe, *The Eight Doors of the Kingdom: Meditations on the Beatitudes* (New York, NY: Scepter Publishers, Inc., 2018), 177-

The single heart, the pure heart, and the merciful heart describe the loving heart. That heart of love, as the quotation indicates, opens the martyr to the whole of creation. He becomes a person concerned with everyone and everything. Nothing is left out of his vision, for he has the eye of an eagle that soars to the heights of love. At the martyr's death, Blessed Mary comes to take him and "ascending with [him] to the Furnace of Love [the Sacred Heart of Jesus], will plunge [him] for all eternity into the burning Abyss of this Love to which [he] has offered [himself] as victim."[93]

---

178. Note that Saint Isaac of Ninevah is also referred to as Isaac the Syrian.

[93] Saint Thérèse of Lisieux, *Story of a Soul*, Translated by John Clarke, O.C.D. (Washington, D.C.: Institute of Carmelite Studies Publications, 1976), Manuscript B Chapter IX "My Vocation is Love," p. 200. Pope Benedict XVI describes compassion as taking up the suffering of the other "in such a way that it becomes mine also. Because it has now become a shared suffering, though, in which another person is present, this suffering is penetrated by the light of love". … [In addition], the capacity to accept suffering for the sake of goodness, truth and justice is an essential criterion of humanity, because if my own well-being and safety are ultimately more important than truth and justice, then the power of the stronger prevails, then violence and untruth reign supreme. Truth and justice must stand above my

Chapter 10: The Transcendental "The One"

The wisdom of Isaac of Ninevah not only captures the concept of a single heart or a merciful heart, but also, he describes something of the martyr's profound charity. For example, the martyr "offers" prayers from the heart "with tears," greatly desiring the conversion of one's brethren. Compassion toward the other, especially the greatest act of mercy for another, the desire that the other reach eternal salvation, aptly describes the martyr's heart. There is no bitterness toward one's persecutors in the heart of the martyr. Rightly, then, is martyrdom described as the "sign of the greatest charity,"[94] for his heart burns with the

---

comfort and physical well-being, or else my life itself becomes a lie" [Benedict XVI, *Spe Salvi*, Vatican translation (Città del Vaticano: Libreria Editrice Vaticana, 2007), 38].

[94] As Aquinas notes, "martyrdom is the greatest proof of the perfection of charity: since a man's love for a thing is proved to be so much the greater, according as that which he despises for its sake is more dear to him, or that which he chooses to suffer for its sake is more odious. But it is evident that of all the goods of the present life man loves life itself most, and on the other hand he hates death more than anything, especially when it is accompanied by the pains of bodily torment.... And from this point of view it is clear that martyrdom is the most perfect of human acts in respect of its genus, as being the sign of the greatest charity..." (Thomas Aquinas, *Summa Theologiae* II-II, 124, 3).

love of God and neighbor, particularly evidenced in the passionate desire that even his enemies "come to the knowledge of the truth" (1 Timothy 2:4).

11

The Transcendental "The True" Illuminates Martyrdom

Next, I consider the transcendental, "the true," in conjunction with the martyr's death. What is truth? The classical definition of truth is the "conformity between what is asserted and what is, or the conformity of intellection with being."[95] As a property of being, the "truth of human intellection depends on being as such; it is caused by being. But being does not...depend on intellection. Being founds intellection; intellection does not found being."[96]

---

[95] Francis Philip O'Farrell, S.J., George Cajetan Reilly, O.P., Michele Paolini Paoletti, Francesca Eustacchi, "Truth" p. 1565-1575 in *New Catholic Encyclopedia Supplement 2012-2013: Ethics and Philosophy*, Ed. Robert L. Fastiggi. Vol IV, 4 vols. (Detroit, MI: Gale, 2013), 1565.

[96] Francis Philip O'Farrell, S.J., George Cajetan Reilly, O.P., Michele Paolini Paoletti, Francesca Eustacchi, "Truth" in *New Catholic Encyclopedia Supplement 2012-2013: Ethics and Philosophy*, 1573.

"Since being as such and the intelligible as such are identical, the act of being (esse) and intelligibility or ontological truth are identical. Hence everything that possesses the act of being, insofar as it does, possesses intelligibility."[97] In other words, whatever exists is intelligible. One can know something about whatever exists. It has an inherent logic, order and harmony such that it can be known to some degree, and it can be understood, again, to some degree. Everything "that is, insofar as it is, is intelligible."[98] For example, a person hiking in the mountains comes upon a creature he has never seen before. His first question is, "What is it"? He strives to know the truth of the creature. Every being is "ontologically true. What is excluded from intelligibility is excluded from

---

[97] Francis Philip O'Farrell, S.J., George Cajetan Reilly, O.P., Michele Paolini Paoletti, Francesca Eustacchi, "Truth" in *New Catholic Encyclopedia Supplement 2012-2013: Ethics and Philosophy*, 1573.

[98] Francis Philip O'Farrell, S.J., George Cajetan Reilly, O.P., Michele Paolini Paoletti, Francesca Eustacchi, "Truth" in *New Catholic Encyclopedia Supplement 2012-2013: Ethics and Philosophy*, 1573.

being."[99] Truth is the proper object of human knowledge.[100]

In the Gospel narrative, Jesus identifies Himself with truth. "I am the Way, and the Truth, and the Life" (John 14:6). Jesus, who is God, is Truth Himself. Even more, all "ontological truth is from God, who knowing Himself knows all that He can will to be, all that can be."[101] God knows Himself and all that exists. He also knows not only all that will come to pass in the future, but also God even knows things that do not exist.[102]

While the demands of the truth might be frightening, "the truth still influences life. Life in fact can

---

[99] Francis Philip O'Farrell, S.J., George Cajetan Reilly, O.P., Michele Paolini Paoletti, Francesca Eustacchi, "Truth" in *New Catholic Encyclopedia Supplement 2012-2013: Ethics and Philosophy*, 1573.

[100] Aristotle, *Metaphysics*, I, 1; Thomas Aquinas, *Summa Theologiae* I, 87, 3, ad. 1 and I, 87, 4 ad. 2.

[101] Francis Philip O'Farrell, S.J., George Cajetan Reilly, O.P., Michele Paolini Paoletti, Francesca Eustacchi, "Truth" in *New Catholic Encyclopedia Supplement 2012-2013: Ethics and Philosophy*, 1575.

[102] Thomas Aquinas, *Summa Contra Gentiles*, Translated by Anton C. Pegis, Edited by Joseph Kenny, O.P. (New York, NY: Hanover House, 1957), I, 66-67.

never be grounded upon doubt, uncertainty or deceit."[103] Applied to martyrdom, one might note that if "the true" concerns the truth of the Faith, then consequently, Faith must inform life regardless of any disadvantages, penalties or costs. Moreover, "the true" is essential because one's act of faith is in God, who is "the guarantor of that truth."[104] Indeed, "the true" highlights and especially focuses upon the Faith, for acting in full freedom, one adheres to the Faith regardless of consequent death.

I have described martyrdom as an act of entrustment to God in the "obedience of faith" above. Here, I highlight John Paul II's explication of that act of entrustment in his Encyclical, *Fides et Ratio*. Specifically, he notes the role of freedom in the person's act.

> In that act [of entrusting oneself to God], the intellect and the will display their spiritual nature, enabling the subject to act in a way which realizes personal freedom to the full.[105]

---

[103] John Paul II, *Fides et Ratio* 28.

[104] John Paul II, *Fides et Ratio* 13.

[105] Here, John Paul II quotes the First Vatican Council, "to which the quotation above refers, [teaching] that the obedience

It is not just that freedom is part of the act of faith: it is absolutely required. Indeed, it is faith that allows individuals to give consummate expression to their own freedom. Put differently, freedom is not realized in decisions made against God. For how could it be an exercise of true freedom to refuse to be open to the very reality which enables our self-realization? Men and women can accomplish no more important act in their lives than the act of faith; it is here that freedom reaches the certainty of truth and chooses to live in that truth.[106]

I note the connection between faith, truth and human freedom. The Holy Father implies that faith is that which is true. Aquinas makes the same point,

---

of faith requires the engagement of the intellect and the will: 'Since human beings are totally dependent on God as their Creator and Lord, and created reason is completely subject to uncreated truth, we are obliged to yield through faith to God the revealer full submission of intellect and will' (Dogmatic Constitution on the Catholic Faith *Dei Filius*, III: *DS* 3008)" quoted in John Paul II, *Fides et Ratio* 13.

[106] John Paul II, *Fides et Ratio* 13.

and his insight connects both the truth and the good to martyrdom.

> [The] martyrs are…witnesses, because by suffering in body unto death they bear witness to the truth; not indeed to any truth, but to the truth which is in accordance with godliness and was made known to us by Christ: wherefore Christ's martyrs are His witnesses. Now this truth is the truth of faith. Wherefore the cause of all martyrdom is the truth of faith.[107]

As Aquinas teaches above, the truth of which the martyr witnesses is the truth of the Faith. One might describe martyrdom, then, as an act of entrustment in faith to God who reveals Himself. Concisely put, martyrdom is entrusting oneself in faith to God unto death.

God is transcendent. He establishes objective truth and one moral law. Highlighting the martyr's death as "true" means one cannot live a lie, for "the capacity to suffer for the sake of the truth is the

---

[107] Thomas Aquinas, *Summa Theologiae* II-II, 124, 5.

Chapter 11: The Transcendental "The True"

measure of humanity."[108] The conscience, which convicts the person and holds him fast, is so strong that one cannot deny the absolute truth to which it testifies. In other words, being a human person signifies being able to transcend the temporal world in which one lives. One has the "capacity to know this transcendent and metaphysical dimension [of reality and truth] in a way that is true and certain," for metaphysics, and thus, the transcendentals, ground the human person "in virtue of their spiritual nature."[109]

I would like to elaborate on Pope Benedict XVI's point that "the capacity to suffer for the sake of the truth is the measure of humanity."[110] The more one is able to "suffer for the sake of the truth" the more "human" one "becomes."[111] I do not mean to say that one is not yet human until one suffers on account of truth, but rather that one "becomes" who he was meant to be in the first place.

The person who learns how to suffer for the truth becomes more simple and more refined. He learns

---

[108] Benedict XVI, *Spe Salvi* 39.
[109] John Paul II, *Fides et Ratio*, 83.
[110] Benedict XVI, *Spe Salvi* 39.
[111] Benedict XVI, *Spe Salvi* 39.

how to love and how to suffer for the sake of the loved one. Again, he becomes more fully who and what he is supposed to be in God's all-wise plan unfolding for him in this postlapsarian world.

Being human means interpersonal communion with others and that requires the willingness to suffer *for*, *with* and *on account of* the other. The martyr is an example of one who shows us this willingness to suffer for the truth and for the One who is loved, namely, God Himself. The pontiff explains that everyone needs "witnesses—martyrs—who have given themselves totally, so as to show us the way—day after day."[112]

> We need them [martyrs] if we are to prefer goodness to comfort, even in the little choices we face each day—knowing that this is how we live life to the full. Let us say it once again: the capacity to suffer for the sake of the truth is the measure of humanity. Yet this capacity to suffer depends on the type and extent of

---

[112] Benedict XVI, *Spe Salvi* 39.

the hope that we bear within us and build upon.[113]

Humanity is only as "human" as it is when humans suffer in order to bear witness to the truth. But suffering on account of the truth of the Gospel is not the end for which one strives. The hope one has, and the hope of the martyr is for eternal life. The level of hope matches one's capacity to suffer – and thus, to love. The martyr's hope for eternal life keeps the goal before the eye of one's mind while he is suffering. As the Liturgy of the Hours describes it, "The martyrs fixed their eyes on heaven, and cried out in their torments: Come, Lord, be with us in this hour."[114]

Truth is so strong that one's whole being is impelled forward to it and by it. A person who knows what is true simply cannot deny that truth in the very core of his being. He might attempt to ignore it, stifle it, or drown it by trying to hold that the opposite is

---

[113] Benedict XVI, *Spe Salvi* 39.

[114] National Conference of Catholic Bishops, *Christian Prayer: The Liturgy of the Hours*, Translated by the International Commission on English in the Liturgy (New York, NY: Catholic Book Publishing Co., 1976), Common of Several Martyrs: Morning Prayer Antiphon 1.

true. In reality, however, thinking or acting contrary to what one knows is true leads to insanity.[115]

Perhaps Joseph Cardinal Ratzinger connects the points together best when he notes the following.

> Whoever believes in God, in the God who revealed Himself precisely in the distorted figure of Christ crucified as Love 'to the end' (John 13:1), knows that beauty is truth and truth beauty; but in the suffering Christ he also learns that the beauty of truth also involves wounds, pain, and even the obscure mystery of death and that this can only be found in accepting pain, not in ignoring it.[116]

---

[115] One might note that several philosophers who regarded themselves as atheists went mad. Friedrich Nietzsche (1844-1900), Georg Wilhelm Friedrich (1770-1831), and Jean-Jacques Rousseau (1712-1778) serve as examples.

[116] Joseph Cardinal Ratzinger, Congregation for the Doctrine of the Faith; Message: To the Communion and Liberation (CL) Meeting at Rimini (24-30 August 2002): *"The Feeling of Things, the Contemplation of Beauty"* in L'Osservatore Romano 34.

Chapter 11: The Transcendental "The True"

Not only is the martyr a witness to the truth of Faith, but also he is the "most authentic witness to the truth about existence" because, in his encounter with Jesus, he has "found the truth about life…; nothing and no-one could ever take this certainty from [him]."[117] The binding power of truth convicts the martyr such that denying Truth (Jesus Christ) is also denying oneself.

Since neither suffering nor death deter one from abandoning "the truth which [he has] discovered in the encounter with Christ," the martyr's witness "continues to arouse such interest" and his "word inspires such confidence: from the moment [he] speak[s] to us of what we perceive deep down as the truth we have sought for so long, the martyrs provide evidence of a love that has no need of lengthy arguments in order to convince."[118] The witness of the martyrs is captivating. It stirs "in us a profound trust because they give voice to what we already feel, and they declare what we would like to have the strength to express."[119]

---

[117] John Paul II, *Fides et Ratio* 32.
[118] John Paul II, *Fides et Ratio* 32.
[119] John Paul II, *Fides et Ratio* 32.

12

What Can "The Good" Say About Martyrdom?

How does the transcendental of "the good" connect to martyrdom?[120] The good is that which all things desire.[121] Moreover, as Saint Thomas explains, "Every being, as being, is good. For all being, as being, has actuality and is in some way perfect; since every act implies some sort of perfection; and perfection implies desirability and goodness."[122]

For example, a bat is a created entity. It is true to the form and matter of "batness," that is, a bat is a flying mammal of the order Chiroptera. While bats carry diseases harmful to people, they also consume insects, which are likewise disease-ridden creatures. Thus, while the bat is certainly not a desirable creature to have as a pet, in its nature, the bat is good. Moreover, it is good in itself and it has a certain

---

[120] Thomas Aquinas, *Summa Theologiae* I, 5, 1.
[121] Thomas Aquinas, *Summa Theologiae* I, 5, 4.
[122] Thomas Aquinas, *Summa Theologiae* I, 5, 4.

perfection (of "batness"), aside from the fact that it eats harmful insects.

While it is gravely immoral to take another person's life in martyrdom, the martyr's act of refusing to deny the Faith and its lived reality (morals) is good. It is an act of worship of God and an act of refusing to live a lie. As noted above, the martyr lays down his life rather than denying Christ and His moral law. One chooses to die rather than to act against the objective order of the good. In sum, one refuses to deny the Commandments.

"The good" teaches that a higher, transcendent law is to be followed at any cost. Since the world continually rebels against a person by tempting him (cf. Matthew 13:22; James 4:4), holding fast to the good requires the virtue of fortitude.

13

Is it Impossible to Attribute Beauty to Martyrdom?

One might wonder whether the transcendental of beauty can relate to martyrdom. For example, beauty radiates a certain order, harmony and proportion. Are those qualities found in martyrdom? Saint Thomas teaches that "[b]eauty and goodness in a thing are identical fundamentally; for they are based upon the same thing, namely, the form; and consequently, goodness is praised as beauty."[123] In this manner, one speaks of the act of a martyr, fidelity to God's holy law unto death, as beautiful. The fidelity, resolution, determination and courage of the martyr radiate his goodness and that goodness is beautiful. In fact, it is a marvel, causing one to wonder in admiration.

To be sure, the actual death itself might cause us to turn aside in horror at the atrocities committed

---

[123] Thomas Aquinas, *Summa Theologiae* I, 5, 4 ad. 1.

against the human person, but the singular fact of a martyr, willing to undergo anything rather than denying Christ or His holy teaching in practice, is not only marvelous, but also, it is beautiful. There is an explicit beauty to his decision. It is ordered according to objective truth and to the objective moral order, which is the ultimate good. The martyr's decision is in harmony with everything he is and knows. Thus, the beautiful is not only "that which pleases upon being seen," but also it describes the metaphysical essence of the martyr's act of the will, which is turned toward the good.[124]

While goodness and beauty are fundamentally identical, Aquinas explains that they differ logically since goodness "relates to the appetite (goodness being what all things desire); and therefore, it has the aspect of an end (the appetite being a kind of movement towards a thing)."[125]

While the good relates to the appetite, Aquinas explains that beauty relates to the cognitive faculty.[126] He enumerates various aspects of beauty as follows.

---

[124] Thomas Aquinas, *Summa Theologiae* I, 5, 4, ad. 1.
[125] Thomas Aquinas, *Summa Theologiae* I, 5, 4 ad. 1.
[126] Thomas Aquinas, *Summa Theologiae* I, 5, 4 ad. 1.

For example, since what is beautiful "pleases when seen," Aquinas concludes that "beauty consists in due proportion; for the senses delight in things duly proportioned."[127]

Connecting Aquinas' thought to the martyr means that his decision to die rather than to forsake Faith or morals is proportionate – to the extent that it *can* be proportionate – to the objective moral order. The martyr does not defy or cast a shadow upon the true or the good, and that proportion between his decision and the good is beautiful.

The beautiful relates to martyrdom not only because of the sheer goodness of the martyr and the beauty of his act of the will, but also because of love, for love is a response to beauty. Aquinas reasons that, "Every agent whatever it be does every action from love of some kind."[128] The martyr, therefore, acts decisively regarding fidelity to God (Faith and morals) because of love. Perceiving something beautiful – God, His truth and His moral law – inspires and so convicts the martyr that he is moved to love. More

---

[127] Thomas Aquinas, *Summa Theologiae* I, 5, 4 ad. 1.
[128] Thomas Aquinas, *Summa Theologiae* I-II, 28, 6.

specifically, love describes beauty as one resting in something in admiration.[129] Beauty brings out the gratuitous aspect of love; it makes one "in-formed," as one is literally taking in the form of something to our being, rendering it a place of hospitality.[130] In sum, beauty deepens and fructifies our love.[131]

Shortly before his martyrdom, Saint Lawrence depicts the sacrificial nature of martyrdom. There is a ritual to it, and that ritual is beautiful insofar as one witnesses the order and harmony of the martyr's steadfastness and determination to be faithful to God and His law. The words I call to mind are these. "You cannot offer sacrifice without a minister."[132] Note the sacrifice to which Lawrence refers. He continues as follows. "Do you not wish that he to whom you gave the Lord's Blood and with whom you have shared the

---

[129] DC Schindler, American Catholic Philosophical Association Conference Paper, "Culture and the Sexual Difference: A Metaphysical Approach" Chicago, Illinois (2024).

[130] DC Schindler, "Culture and the Sexual Difference: A Metaphysical Approach" (2024).

[131] DC Schindler, "Culture and the Sexual Difference: A Metaphysical Approach" (2024).

[132] Ambrose, *De Officiis* in Moraglia, "Saint Lawrence Proto-Deacon of the Roman Church."

Sacred Mysteries should spill his own blood with you?"[133] Thus, the sacred ritual of martyrdom imitates, in a very small way, the Sacrifice of Christ on the Cross perpetuated throughout time in the Holy Sacrifice of the Mass.

---

[133] Ambrose, *De Officiis* in Moraglia, "Saint Lawrence Proto-Deacon of the Roman Church."

14

The Metaphysics of Martyrdom

It remains to summarize the specific connections between the transcendentals of the one, the true, the good and the beautiful to martyrdom, itself. What do the transcendentals teach about martyrdom? In turn, one might ponder what martyrdom teaches about being, man, and God.

To the people of our own day, the concept of martyrdom dictates a whole new understanding of being, the human person, and God Himself. The metaphysical meaning of martyrdom, explicated with the assistance of the transcendentals, describes being—reality itself—as transcendent. The martyr testifies to the fact that each person is not created simply for being in this world. There is a greater End for which each person is created and toward which one ought to strive with the entirety of one's heart, soul and mind (cf. Matthew 22:37), for nothing is worth more than reaching the Beatific Vision of God (cf. Matthew 16:24-26).

Eternal life is worth every and any sacrifice, deprivation or act of self-denial needed to get there. Courage, willingness to suffer, and the hope of eternal life are to be our daily praxes, structuring the art of living well. It makes a difference whether one prays. What one believes is the anchor that grounds one's vision of reality. If it is *right* faith, it is objectively true. Thus, nothing should cause a person to forfeit or abandon the true Faith (Catholicism). In addition, following the Commandments shapes the pattern of one's life in accord with the ultimate good and obedience "unto death" (Philippians 2:8). Finally, beauty sums up a life lived in sacrificial love for others. It is the compass that orders and harmonizes life to its proper proportion. It points to ritual and right worship, just as the ancient Israelites were taught by God how to worship rightly in the desert.

One might reasonably conclude, then, that the person—here, the martyr—does indeed constitute "a privileged locus for the encounter with being," for it is when one "discover[s] a call to the absolute and transcendent [that] the metaphysical dimension of reality opens up before [him]: in truth, in beauty, in moral values, in other persons, in being itself, in

God."[134] Thus, rightly does one articulate martyrdom as the art of both living well and dying well.

In order to die well, how must one live? I would like to propose an answer to this question with the following Scripture passage and offer it as a summary of the metaphysics of martyrdom.

In the Book of Acts we read, "And they were persevering in the doctrine of the apostles, and in the communication of the breaking of bread, and in prayers" (Acts 2:42 DRA). In the RSVCE translation, one reads as follows. "And they devoted themselves to the apostles' teaching [Creed, truth] and fellowship [Commandments, the good], to the breaking of bread [sacraments, beauty] and the prayers" (Acts 2:42). From Acts 2, then, we have four points, or the four "pillars" of the Faith: Creed ("the doctrine of the apostles"), Commandments ("fellowship"), the sacraments ("the breaking of bread") and prayer ("prayers").

These four points, prayer (the one), Creed (the true), Commandments (the good) and worship (the beautiful) flow from the metaphysical description of

---

[134] John Paul II, *Fides et Ratio* 83.

martyrdom. They also align with the four pillars of the *Catechism of the Catholic Church*, though in a slightly different order: Creed (the true), sacraments (the beautiful), Commandments (the good) and prayer (the one). A chart serves to clarify.

Transcendental	Pillar of the Church	Words of Acts 2:42	Martyrdom
True	Creed	the doctrine of the apostles	entrust self in faith & freedom unto death
Good	Commandments	fellowship	right action, prudence, charity
Beauty	Sacraments	the breaking of bread	ritual and worship of God
One	Prayer	prayers	single heartedness

I have described martyrdom as single heartedness (prayer, which corresponds with the transcendental, "the one"), which in turn corresponds to the

Chapter 14: The Metaphysics of Martyrdom

prayer of the early Christians in Acts 2. Single heartedness, or prayer (corresponds to the one) demands the charitable heart filled with love of God and neighbor, which can only come through God's grace, faithful reception of the sacraments, ardent prayer, following the Commandments (including virtuous living) and the willingness to suffer for the truth. As Saint Paul teaches, "There is one body and one Spirit, just as you were called to the one hope that belongs to your call, one Lord, one faith, one baptism, one God and Father of us all, who is above all and through all and in all" (Ephesians 4:4-6).

I have also depicted martyrdom as entrusting oneself in faith unto death, and that corresponds to the truth. It is akin to the Creed, doctrine, or "the teaching of the Apostles," as noted in Acts 2, for the martyr "speaks" the truth with his free-will decision at the moment of death.

Martyrdom elucidated with the transcendental "the good" matches the Commandments. In turn, the Decalogue corresponds to the good, for "to inherit eternal life" one follows the law of the Lord, which is inscribed in the Decalogue (Luke 10:25-28). When one follows the Commandments, he lives in harmony and "fellowship" with one another.

Finally, ritual and worship, such as the liturgy, correspond to beauty, and to "the breaking of the bread," as Acts 2 describes. Recall the words of Saint Lawrence, in which he compares the "ritual" of martyrdom to the Holy Sacrifice of the Mass. As noted above, Lawrence addresses Pope Saint Sixtus II in terms that denote sacrifice. Just as he served the Pope during the Mass as a Deacon, so also, he wishes to serve him by joining him in making the ultimate sacrifice of life. "'Where do you hasten to, holy Bishop, without your Deacon? You cannot offer sacrifice without a minister. ... Do you not wish that he to whom you gave the Lord's Blood and with whom you have shared the Sacred Mysteries should spill his own blood with you?"[135]

In sum, Faith (corresponds to truth) as that act of entrustment to God requires belief, which is a rich human experience "because it involves an interpersonal relationship;" it "brings into play not only a

---

[135] Ambrose, *De Officiis* in Moraglia, "Saint Lawrence Proto-Deacon of the Roman Church."

person's capacity to know but also the deeper capacity to entrust oneself to others, to enter into a relationship with them which is intimate and enduring."[136] One must not only *know* God, but *believe* in Him and in His love for him (cf. 1 John 4:8, 16). Following the Commandments (corresponds to right action in accord with the good) and worship of God (corresponds to beauty) also describe the way life is to be lived.

---

[136] John Paul II, *Fides et Ratio* 32.

15

The Martyr's Vision of Reality

We return to our preliminary question. What vision of reality does the martyr manifest? Technology has been dubbed, the ontology of our age.[137] In other words, the West "has ever-more pervasively conflated knowing—that is, the human being's original presence to and in the world—with making."[138] Further, this "presence-as-making" is missing "an anterior sense of presence-as-being-given: of being, ours and the world's, as a gift."[139] God's created beings—everything He has created—have been given to each person as a gift.

Saint Bonaventure differentiates between theology and philosophy, faith and reason, in a way that enlightens my inquiry and brings it into focus.

---

[137] George Grant, *Technology and Justice* (Toronto, ON: Anansi, 1986). George Grant, *Lament for a Nation* (Princeton, NJ: Van Nostrand, 1965), 11. "As Heidegger has said, technique is the metaphysic of the age" (11).

[138] Schindler, *Ordering Love*, 277-278.

[139] Schindler, *Ordering Love*, 278.

Specifically, he highlights *love* as the motivating impulse in one's search for truth.[140] Connecting the quest for truth to the action of the martyr's death, I again recall that martyrdom has long been identified as the supreme act of charity. "Greater love has no man than this, that a man lay down his life for his friends" (John 15:13). In addition, from Isaac of Ninevah, one learns that the martyr's heart "burns unto the whole of creation" with charity toward God and neighbor. In my analysis above, I especially highlight love of enemies. What the martyr's lesson signifies is that each day one is to strive for charity, especially as understood in forgiveness from the heart and love of one's enemy (cf. Matthew 6:14-15; Luke 6:27). Moreover, the martyr witnesses to love imbued by Faith. Ratzinger connects love and Faith as follows.

> Faith can wish to understand because it is moved by love for the one upon whom it has bestowed its consent. Love seeks understand-

---

[140] I might note, then, that the genuine search for truth is impelled by love and not by curiosity. Although it would need to be developed elsewhere, one might argue that curiosity instigates a seemingly endless desire for information.

ing; it wishes to know ever better the one whom it loves. It seeks His Face as Augustine never tires of repeating. Love is the desire for intimate knowledge, so that the quest for intelligence can even be an inner requirement of love. ... Yet love for Christ and of one's neighbor for Christ's sake can enjoy stability and consistency only if it its deepest motivation is love for the truth.[141]

While one often describes a person according to what he does in life, such as a shoemaker or a banker, the martyr is described by the moment of his death: "...in truth, only someone who comes from Christ can be open to the people of today. Man is ordered to God in time and eternity. Only someone who acknowledges Christ as the mediator between God and mankind can accomplish something positive and

---

[141] Joseph Cardinal Ratzinger, *Nature and Mission of Theology*, 27. Love seeks the face of Christ.

constructive for the world, society, and the Church in the light of divine truth."[142]

The martyrs bring forth life and an increase of members for the Mystical Body. As Tertullian once famously said, "The more you mow us down, the more we grow: the blood of the martyrs is the seed of the Christians."[143] The fidelity of one person to Jesus Christ unto death brings forth the fruit of many others. "Man cannot grasp how death could be the source of life and love; yet to reveal the mystery of his saving plan God has chosen precisely that which reason considers 'foolishness' and a 'scandal.'"[144]

The martyr's vision of reality, then, is keeping both eyes fixed on the goal, which is eternal life. The whole of being, which is created by God, is imbued with love, for it is meant to draw one toward that blessed eternity. God is the ultimate Being, who is One (cf. Deuteronomy 6:4), True (cf. John 14:6) and Good (cf. Matthew 19:16-17; Mark 10:17-18; Luke

---

[142] Gerhard Müller, *The Power of Truth: The Challenges to Catholic Doctrine and Morals Today* (San Francisco, CA: Ignatius Press, 2019), 10.

[143] Tertullian, *Apologeticum*, 50, 13: Jacques Paul Minge, *Patrologia Latina* 1, 534.

[144] John Paul II, *Fides et Ratio* 23.

18:18-19). Indeed, He is Beauty, Himself, for "no eye has seen, nor ear heard, nor the heart of man conceived, what God has prepared for those who love Him" (1 Corinthians 2:9). The martyr makes known that the "one thing" he asks is to "dwell in the house of the Lord" (Psalm 27:4), for this is the "one thing" (Luke 10:42) that endures forever: loving in the presence of Love, Himself (cf. 1 Corinthians 13:13).

The timeless martyrs of the ages speak to the human race of all times and places. Their witness "continues to arouse such interest, to draw agreement, to win such a hearing and to invite emulation."[145] Why does the martyr inspire one so much?

> This is why their word inspires such confidence: from the moment they speak to us of what we perceive deep down as the truth we have sought for so long, the martyrs provide evidence of a love that has no need of lengthy arguments in order to convince. The martyrs stir in us a profound trust because they give voice to what we already feel, and they declare

---

[145] John Paul II, *Fides et Ratio* 32.

what we would like to have the strength to express.[146]

Let us not hide the truth of Jesus Christ "from the world out of cowardice and deny the Lord out of human respect."[147] Instead, let us go forward in "confidence and love," entirely convinced that the Father in Heaven loves the prodigal child He calls to His side.[148]

---

[146] John Paul II, *Fides et Ratio* 32.

[147] Gerhard Müller, *The Power of Truth*, 10.

[148] Saint Thérèse of the Child Jesus and of the Holy Face, *Story of a Soul*, 259.

> "Misericordias Domini
> in aeternum cantabo."
>
> Psalm 88:2

Bibliography

Adler, Mortimer J. *Six Great Ideas*. New York, NY: Touchstone Simon & Schuster Inc. 1997.

Aertsen, Jan A. "Beauty in the Middle Ages: A Forgotten Transcendental?" in *Medieval Philosophy & Theology* Vol. 1 pages 68-97. 1991. https://doi.org/10.5840/medievalpt199115.

Aertsen, Jan A. and Wouter Goris. "Transcendentals" Vol. 4 pages 1556-1560 in *New Catholic Encyclopedia Supplement 2012-2013: Ethics and Philosophy*. Ed. Robert L. Fastiggi. 4 vols. Detroit, MI: Gale. 2013.

Ambrose. *De Officiis* in Fr. Francesco Moraglia, "Saint Lawrence Proto-Deacon of the Roman Church." https://press.vatican.va/roman_curia/congregations/cclergy/documents/rc_con_cclergy_doc_19022000_slaw_en.html.

Aquinas, Thomas. *Questiones Disputatae de Veritate: Truth*. Translated by James V. McGlynn, S.J. Chicago, IL: Henry Regnery Company, 1953. https://isidore.co/aquinas/QDdeVer17.htm.

---. *Summa Contra Gentiles*. Translated by Anton C. Pegis. Edited by Joseph Kenny, O.P. New York, NY: Hanover House. 1957.

---. *Summa Theologiae*. Translated by the Fathers of the English Dominican Province. Vol. 3 (5 Vols.) Westminster, MD: Christian Classics. 1981.

---. *Summa Theologiae*. Torino: Edizioni San Paolo. 1999.

Aristotle. *Categories, Metaphysics, Politics, Rhetoric* in *Basic Works of Aristotle*. Edited by Richard McKeon. New York, NY: Random House, 1941.

Augustine of Hippo. *Confessions*. Ignatius Critical Editions. Translated by Maria Boulding, O.S.B. Edited by David Vincent Meconi, S.J. Series Editor Joseph Pearce. San Francisco, CA: Ignatius Press. 2012.

Baker, S.J., Kenneth. *Fundamentals of Catholicism*. Vol 3 (4 Vols.) San Francisco, CA: Ignatius Press. 1983.

Bibliorum Sacrorum. Iuxta Vulgatam Clementinam. Nova Editio. Aloisius Gramatica. Typis Polyglottis Vaticanis. 1959.

Burns, Tony. *Aristotle and Natural Law*. New York, NY: Continuum. 2011.

Canons and Decrees of the Council of Trent, The. Translated and Introduced by H. J. Schroeder, O.P. Rockford: Tan Books and Publishers, Inc. 1978.

Catechism of the Catholic Church, Second Edition. Washington, D.C.: United States Catholic Conference, Inc. Libreria Editrice Vaticana. 1997.

Catechismus Catholicae Ecclesiae. Citta del Vaticano: Libreria Editrice Vaticana. 1997.

Dahlstrom, Daniel O. and Marco Lamanna. "Ontology" Vol. 3 pages 1103 in *New Catholic Encyclopedia Supplement 2012-2013: Ethics and Philosophy*. Ed. Robert L. Fastiggi. 4 vols. Detroit, MI: Gale. 2013.

Flannery, O.P., Austin. General Editor. *Vatican Council II, Vol. 1: The Conciliar and Post Conciliar Documents*, New Revised Edition. *Dei Verbum*; *Gaudium et Spes*; *Lumen Gentium*. Northport, NY: Costello Publishing Co. 1996.

Grant, George. *Lament for a Nation*. Princeton, NJ: Van Nostrand. 1965.

---. *Technology and Justice*. Toronto: Anansi. 1986.

Hardon, S.J., John A. *Catholic Dictionary*. New York, NY: Image Books. 2013.

---. *Modern Catholic Dictionary*. Garden City, NY: Doubleday & Company, Inc. 1980.

Holy Bible, The. Douay Rheims Version. Revised by Bishop Richard Challoner 1749-1752. Rockford, IL: Tan Books and Publishers, Inc. 1989.

Holy Bible, The. Revised Standard Version Catholic Edition. https://www.biblegateway.com.

Holy Bible, The. Revised Standard Version Second Catholic Edition. San Francisco, CA: Thomas Nelson Publishing for Ignatius Press. 2006.

Ignatius of Antioch. *Early Christian Writings: The Apostolic Fathers*. Translated by Maxwell Staniforth. New York, NY: Dorset Press. 1986.

Jerusalem Bible, The. Alexander Jones, L.S.S., S.T.L., I.C.B., General Editor. Garden City, NY: Doubleday & Company, Inc. 1966.

John Paul II. *Fides et Ratio*. Vatican Translation. Boston, MA: Pauline Books and Media. 1998.

---. *Veritatis Splendor*. Vatican Translation. Boston, MA: Saint Paul Books and Media. 1993.

Kovach, Francis J. and Margaret I. Hughes. "Beauty as a Transcendental" Vol. 1 pages 162-166 in *New Catholic Encyclopedia Supplement 2012-2013:*

Ethics and Philosophy. Ed. Robert L. Fastiggi. 4 vols. Detroit, MI: Gale. 2013.

McInerny, Ralph M. and Jeffrey Dirk Wilson. "Being" Vol. 1 pages 169-175 in *New Catholic Encyclopedia Supplement 2012-2013: Ethics and Philosophy*. Ed. Robert L. Fastiggi. 4 vols. Detroit, MI: Gale. 2013.

Miller, Anthony Michael. "The Transcendental Status of Beauty: Evaluating the Debate among Neo-Thomistic Philosophers." *Religions* 15, no. 10: 1207 (2024). https://doi.org/10.3390/rel15101207.

Müller, Gerhard. *The Power of Truth: The Challenges to Catholic Doctrine and Morals Today*. San Francisco, CA: Ignatius Press. 2019.

Murphy, S.J., James G. "Metaphysics" Vol. 3 page 1186 in *New Catholic Encyclopedia Supplement 2012-2013: Ethics and Philosophy*. Ed. Robert L. Fastiggi. 4 vols. Detroit, MI: Gale. 2013.

National Conference of Catholic Bishops. *Christian Prayer: The Liturgy of the Hours*. Translated by the International Commission on English in the Liturgy. New York, NY: Catholic Book Publishing Company. 1976.

New American Bible, The. Nashville, TN: Catholic Bible Press Thomas Nelson Publishers. 1987.

Novum Testamentum Graece. Nestle-Aland. Stuttgart: Deutsche Bibelgesellschaft. 1898 und 1993.

O'Farrell, S.J., Francis Philip and George Cajetan Reilly, O.P., Michele Paolini Paoletti, Francesca Eustacchi. "Truth" Vol. 4 pages 1565-1575 in *New Catholic Encyclopedia Supplement 2012-2013: Ethics and Philosophy*. Ed. Robert L. Fastiggi. 4 vols. Detroit, MI: Gale. 2013.

Philippe, Jacques. *The Eight Doors of the Kingdom: Meditations on the Beatitudes*. New York, NY: Scepter Publishers, Inc. 2018.

Plato. *Apology*, *Phaedo*, *Cratylus*, and *Republic* in *The Collected Dialogues of Plato Including the Letters*. Bollingen Series LXXI. Edited by Edith Hamilton and Huntington Cairns. Translated by Hugh Tredennick, et al. Princeton, NJ: Princeton University Press. 1980.

Ratzinger, Joseph / Benedict XVI. *Spe Salvi*. Vatican translation. Città del Vaticano: Libreria Editrice Vaticana. 2007.

Ratzinger, Joseph. Congregation for the Doctrine of the Faith. Message: To the Communion and

Liberation (CL) Meeting at Rimini (24-30 August 2002). "*The Feeling of Things, the Contemplation of Beauty*" in L'Osservatore Romano.

---. *The Nature and Mission of Theology: Essays to Orient Theology in Today's Debates*. Translated by Adrian Walker. San Francisco, CA: Ignatius Press. 1995.

Reimers, Adrian J. *Truth About the Good: Moral Norms in the Thought of John Paul II*. Ave Maria, FL: Sapientia Press of Ave Maria University. 2011.

Sacrosanctum Oecumenicum Concilium Vaticanum II: Constitutiones Decreta Declarationes. Dei Verbum; Gaudium et Spes; Lumen Gentium. Citta Del Vaticano: Libreria Editrice Vaticana. 1993.

Schindler, David C. American Catholic Philosophical Association Conference Paper. "Culture and the Sexual Difference: A Metaphysical Approach." Chicago, Illinois. 2024.

---. "Love and Beauty: The 'Forgotten Transcendental' in Thomas Aquinas" *Communio: International Catholic Review* 44 (Summer 2017).

---. The Edna and George McMahon Aquinas Lecture (2016). YouTube, https://www.youtube.com/watch?v=ei6eRK28oac.

Schindler, David L. *Ordering Love: Liberal Societies and the Memory of God*. Grand Rapids and Cambridge: William B. Eerdmans Publishing Company. 2011.

Siegmund, J. Marianne. *The Face of Jesus, the Martyr, and the Reciprocity of Abiding Love: Anthropological Considerations in Spiritual Theology Based Upon the Pontifical Writings of Pope Saint John Paul the Great*. Saint Louis, MO: En Route Books and Media, 2024.

Tertullian. *Apologeticum*, 50, 13 in Jacques Paul Minge. *Patrologiae Cursus Completus, Series Latina*. Apud Garnier Fratres, Editores et J.-P. Migne Successores. Parisiis: 1880.

Thérèse of Lisieux. *Story of a Soul*. Translated by John Clarke, O.C.D. Washington, D.C.: Institute of Carmelite Studies Publications. 1976.

Wouter, Goris and Jan Aertsen. "Medieval Theories of Transcendentals" in *The Stanford Encyclopedia of Philosophy*. (Fall 2019 Edition). Edward N. Zalta, Editor. https://plato.stanford.edu/archives/fall2019/entries/transcendentals-medieval/, 7.